The

Strangest Secret

By
Earl Nightingale

&

As A Man Thinketh

By
James Allen

Table *of* Contents

The Strangest Secret

As A Man Thinketh

The
Strangest Secret

Earl Nightingale

Text *of the Audio* Version

I'd like to tell you about The Strangest Secret in the World. The late Nobel prize-winning Dr. Albert Schweitzer was once asked, "Doctor, what is wrong with men today?" The great doctor was silent a moment, and then he said, "Men simply do not think!" It is about this that I want to talk with you.

We live today in a golden age. This is an era that humanity has looked forward to, dreamed of, and worked toward for thousands of years. But since it is here, we pretty well take it for granted. We are fortunate to live in the richest era that ever existed on the face of the earth. A land of abundant opportunity for everyone. But do you know what happens?

Let's take 100 individuals who start even at the age of 25. Do you have any idea what will happen to those men and women by the time they are 65?

These 100 people, who all start even at the age of 25, all believe they're going to be successful. If you ask any one of them if they want to be a success, they would tell you they did. You would notice that they are eager toward life, there is a certain sparkle in their eye, an erectness to their carriage. Life seems like a pretty interesting adventure to them.

But by the time they are 65, only one will be rich, four will be financially independent, 41 will still be working, and 54 will be broke - depending on others for life's necessities.

Now think a moment: Out of the 100, only five make the grade!
* Why do so many fail?
* What has happened to the sparkle that was there when they were 25?
* What has become of their dreams, their hopes, their plans?
* Why is there such a large disparity between what these people intended to do and what they actually accomplished?

The Definition *of* Success

When we say about 5% achieve success, we have to define success. Here is the best definition I've ever been able to find: *"Success is the progressive realization of a worthy ideal."*

If someone is working toward a predetermined goal and knows where they are going, that person is a success. If they are not doing that, they are a failure.

"Success is the progressive realization of a worthy ideal."

Rollo May, the distinguished psychiatrist, wrote in his wonderful book called: "Man's Search for Himself". *"The opposite of courage in our society is not cowardice - it is conformity."*

And there you have the trouble today; the reason for so many failures. Conformity... people acting like everyone else, without knowing why or without knowing where they are going.

Now think of it. Right now in America, there are over 40 million people 65 years of age and older. And most of them are broke. They are dependent on someone else for life's necessities.

- We learn to read by the time we are seven.
- We learn to make a living by the time we're 25.
- Often by that time we are not only making a living, we're supporting a family.
- And yet by the time we are 65, we have not learned how to become financially independent in the richest land that has ever been known.

Why? We conform. The trouble is most of us are acting like the wrong percentage group - the 95 who do not succeed.

Why do people conform? Well, they really don't know. Most people seem to believe their lives are shaped by circumstances, by things that happen to them by exterior forces. They are outer directed people.

A survey was made one time that covered a lot of people, working people. These people were asked, "Why do you work?" "Why do you get up in the morning?" 19 out of 20 had no idea.

If you press them they will say, "Everyone goes to work in the morning." And that is the reason they do it - because everyone else is doing it.

Now let's get back to our definition of success. Who succeeds? The only person who succeeds is the person who is progressively realizing a worthy ideal. It is the person who says, "I am going to become this", and then begins to work towards that goal.

I'll tell you the successful people are.

- A success is the school teacher who is teaching school because that's what he or she wants to do.
- A success is the woman who is a wife and mother because she wanted to become a wife and mother and is doing a good job of it.
- A success is the man who runs the corner gas station because that was his dream.
- A success is the entrepreneur who starts their own company because that was their dream - that's what they wanted to do.
- A success is the successful salesperson who wants to become a top-notch salesperson and grow and build with in his or her organization and sets forth on the pursuit of that goal.

A success is anyone who is pursuing deliberately a predetermined goal, because that's what he or she decided to do ... deliberately. But only one out of 20 does that. The rest are "failures."

That is why today there is really not any competition unless we make it for ourselves. Instead of competing, all we have to do is create.

For twenty years I looked for the key which would determine what would happen to a human being. I wanted to know if there was a key that would make the future a promise that we could foretell to a large extent.

Was there a key that would guarantee a person's becoming successful if they only knew about it and knew how to use it? *Well there is such a key and I have found it.*

Goals

Have you ever wondered why so many people work so hard and honestly without ever achieving anything in particular? And why others don't seem to work hard, yet seem to get everything? They seem to have the "magic touch." You've heard people say about someone, "Everything he touches turns to gold."

Have you ever noticed that a person who becomes successful tends to continue to become more successful? On the other hand, have you noticed how someone who is a failure tends to continue to fail?

The difference is goals. Some of us have goals, some don't. People with goals succeed because they know where they are going.

It's that simple.

Failures, on the other hand, believe that their lives are shaped by circumstances... by things that happen to them... by exterior forces.

Think of a ship leaving a harbor. Think of it with the complete voyage mapped out and planned. The captain and crew know exactly where the ship is going and how long it will take - it has a definite goal. And 9,999 times out of 10,000, it will get to where it started out to get.

Now let's take another ship, just like the first, only let's not put a crew on it, or a captain at the helm. Let's give it no aiming point, no goal, and no destination. We just start the engines and let it go. I think you'll agree with me that if it gets out of the harbor at all, it will either sink or wind up on some deserted beach - a derelict. It can't go any place because it has no destination and no guidance.

It's the same with a human being.

Take the salesman for example. There is no other person in the world today with the future of a good salesperson! Selling is the world's highest paid profession, if you are good at it and if you know where you are going. Every company needs top notched salespeople. And they reward those people, the sky is the limit for them. But how many can you find?

Someone once said the human race is fixed. Not to prevent the strong from winning, but to prevent the weak from losing.

Western society today can be likened to a naval convoy in time of war. The entire economy is slowed down to protect its weakest link, just as the convoy has to go at the speed that will permit its slowest vessel to remain in formation.

That's why it's so easy to make a living today. It takes no particular brains or talent to make a living and support a family today. We have a plateau of so-called "security", if that is what a person is looking for. But we all do have to decide how high above this plateau we want to aim.

Now let's get back to the Strangest Secret in The World, the story I wanted to tell you today.

Why do those with goals succeed in life, and those without them fail? Well let me tell you something which, if you really understand it, will alter your life immediately. If you understand completely what I'm about to tell you from this moment on, your life will never be the same again.

You will suddenly find that good luck just seems to be attracted to you. The things you want just seem to fall in line. And from now on you won't have the problems, the worries, the gnawing lump of anxiety that perhaps you have experienced before. Doubt and fear will now be things of the past.

Here is the key to success, and, the key to failure.

"We become what we think about".

Let me say that again.

"We become what we think about".

Throughout history, the great wise men and teachers, philosophers, and prophets have disagreed with one another on many different things. It is only on this one point that they are in complete and unanimous agreement - the key to success and the key to failure is this:

"We become what we think about".

Listen to what Marcus Aurelius, the great Roman Emperor, said: "A man's life is what his thoughts make of it." Benjamin Disraeli said this: "Everything comes if a man will only wait... I've brought myself, by long meditation, to the conviction that a human being with a settled purpose must accomplish it, and nothing can resist a will which will stake even existence upon its fulfillment."

Ralph Waldo Emerson said this, "A man is what he thinks about all day long."

William James said: "The greatest discovery of my generation is that human beings can alter their lives by altering their attitudes of mind."

And he said, "We need only in cold blood act as if the thing in question were real, and it will become infallibly real by growing into such a connection with our life that it will become real. It will become so knit with habit and emotion that our interests in it will be those which characterize belief."

He also said,

- "If you only care enough for a result, you will almost certainly obtain it."
- "If you wish to be rich, you will be rich."
- "If you wish to be learned, you will be learned."
- "If you wish to be good, you will be good."

He continues though, "... only you must, then, really wish these things, and wish them exclusively, and not wish at the same time a hundred other incompatible things just as strongly."

In the Bible you will read in Mark 9-23:

"If thou canst believe, all things are possible to him that believeth."

My old friend Dr. Norman Vincent Peale put it this way:

"This is one of the greatest laws in the universe. Fervently do I wish I had discovered it as a very young man. It dawned upon me much later in life, and I found it to be the greatest discovery, if not my greatest discovery outside my relationship to God."

The great law briefly and simply stated is:

- "If you think in negative terms, you will get negative results."
- "If you think in positive terms, you will achieve positive results."

"That simple fact," he went on to say, "is the basis of an astonishing law of prosperity and success." In three words:

"Believe and Succeed."

William Shakespeare put it this way, "Our doubts are traitors and make us lose the good we oft might win by fearing to attempt."

George Bernard Shaw said:

"People are always blaming their circumstances for what they are. I don't believe in circumstances. The people who get on in this world are the people who get up and look for the circumstances they want, and if they can't find them, make them.

Well, it's pretty apparent, isn't it? And every person who discovered this, for a while, believed that they were the first to work it out.

"We become what we think about."

It stands to reason that a person who is thinking about a concrete and worthwhile goal is going to reach it, because that's what he's thinking about. And we become what we think about.

Conversely, the person who has no goal, who doesn't know where they are going, and whose thoughts must therefore be thoughts of confusion, anxiety, fear, and worry becomes what they think about. Their life becomes one of frustration, fear, anxiety, and worry.

And if we think about nothing ... we become nothing.

Now how does it work?

Why do we become what we think about?

Well, I'll tell you how it works as far as we know. To do this I want to talk about a situation that parallels the human mind.

As Ye Sow, So Shall Ye Reap

The human mind is much like a farmer's land.

Suppose a farmer has some land. And it is good fertile land. The land gives the farmer a choice. He may plant in that land whatever he chooses. The land doesn't care what is planted. It's up to the farmer to make the decision.

Remember we are comparing the human mind to the farmers land because, the mind, like the land, doesn't care what you plant in it. It will return what you plant, but it doesn't care what you plant.

Let's say that the farmer has two seeds in his hand - one a seed of corn, the other is nightshade, a deadly poison. He digs two little holes in the earth and he plants both seeds, one corn, the other nightshade.

He covers up the holes, waters, and takes care of the land. What will happen? Invariably, the land will return what is planted. As it is written in the Bible, "*As ye sow, so shall ye reap.*"

Remember, the land doesn't care. It will return poison in just as wonderful abundance as it will corn. So up come the two plants - one corn, one poison. The human mind is far more fertile, far more incredible and mysterious than the land, but it works the same way. It does not care what we plant... success... or failure. A concrete, worthwhile goal... or confusion, misunderstanding, fear, anxiety, and so on. But what we plant it must return to us.

The human mind is the last great unexplored continent on earth. It contains riches beyond our wildest dreams. It will return anything we want to plant.

So you may say, if that is true, why don't people use their minds more? Well I think they've figured out an answer to that one too.

The problem is that our mind comes as standard equipment at birth. It's free. And things that are given to us for nothing, we place little value on. Things that we pay money for, we value.

The paradox is that exactly the reverse is true. Everything that's really worthwhile in life came to us free: our minds, our souls, our bodies, our hopes, our dreams, our ambitions, our intelligence, our love of family and children and friends and country. All these priceless possessions are free.

But the things that cost us money are actually very cheap and can be replaced at any time. A good man can be completely wiped out and make another fortune. He can do that several times. Even if our home burns down, we can rebuild it. But the things we got for nothing, we can never replace.

The human mind is not used because we take it for granted. "Familiarity breeds contempt". It can do any kind of job we assign to it, but generally speaking, we use it for little jobs instead of big important ones. Universities have proved that most of us are operating on about ten percent or less of our abilities.

So decide now.

What is it you want?

Plant your goal in your mind.

It's the most important decision you'll ever make in your entire life.

What is it you want?
- Do you want to be an outstanding salesman?
- Do you want to excel at your particular job?
- Do you want to go places in your company? ... in your community?
- Do you want to be rich?

All you have got to do is plant that seed in your mind, care for it, work steadily towards your goal, and it will become a reality.

It not only will, there's no way that it cannot. You see, that's a law - like the laws of Sir Isaac Newton, the laws of gravity. If you get on top of a building and jump off, you'll always go down - you'll never go up. And it's the same with all the other laws of nature.

They are inflexible.

They always work.

Think about your goal in a relaxed, positive way. Picture yourself in your mind's eye as having already achieved this goal. See yourself doing the things you will be doing when you have reached your goal.

Ours has been called a Phenobarbital Age, the age of ulcers and nervous breakdowns and tranquilizers at a time when medical research has raised us to a new plateau of good health and longevity, far too many of us worry ourselves into an early grave trying to cope with things in our own little personal ways, without learning a few great laws that will take care of everything for us.

These things we bring on ourselves through our habitual way of thinking. Every one of us is the sum total of our own thoughts.

We are where we are because that is exactly where we really want or feel we deserve to be - whether we'll admit that or not.

Each of us must live off the fruit of our thoughts in the future, because what you think today and tomorrow - next month and next year - will mold your life and determine your future. You are guided by your mind.

I remember one time I was driving through eastern Arizona. I saw one of those giant earth-moving machines roaring along the road at about 35 miles an hour with what looked like 30 tons of dirt in it - a tremendous, incredible machine - and there was a little man perched way up on top with the wheel in his hands, guiding it. As I drove along I was struck by the similarity of that machine to the human mind.

Just suppose you are sitting at the controls of such a vast source of energy. Are you going to sit back and fold your arms and let it run itself into a ditch? Or are you going to keep both hands firmly on the wheel and control and direct this power to a specific, worthwhile purpose? It's up to you.

You are in the driver's seat.

You see, the very law that gives us success is a double-edged sword. We must control our thinking. The same rule that can lead people to lives of success, wealth, happiness, and all the things they ever dreamed of for themselves and their family

That very same law can lead them into the gutter.

It's all in how it is used: for success... or for failure.

This is The Strangest Secret in the world.

Why do I say it's strange, and why do I call it a secret? Actually, it is not a secret at all.

It was first promulgated by some of the earliest wise men, and it appears again and again throughout the Bible. But very few people have learned it or understand it. That's why it's strange, and why for some equally strange reason it virtually remains a secret.

I believe you could go out and walk down the main street of your town and ask one person after another what the secret of success is and you probably would not run into one person in a month that could tell you. This information is enormously valuable to us if we really understand it and apply it. It is valuable to us not only for our own lives, but the lives of those around us, our families, employees, associates, and friends.

Life should be an exciting adventure.

It should never be a bore.

A person should work fully, be alive. You should be glad to get out of bed in the morning. You should be doing a job that you like to do because you do it well.

One time I heard Grove Patterson, the great late editor in chief of the Toledo Daily Blade make a speech. And as he concluded his speech he said something I've never forgotten. He said, "My years in the newspaper business have convinced me of several things. Among them, that people are basically good, and that we came from someplace and we are going someplace. So we should make our time here an exciting adventure. The architect of the universe did not build a stairway leading nowhere. The greatest teacher of all, the carpenter from the

Plains of Galilee of all gave us the secret time and time again: As ye believe, so shall it be done - unto you."

30 Day Action Ideas *for* Putting
The Strangest Secret *to* Work *for* You

I've explained the Strangest Secret in the World, and how it works. Now I'd like to explain how you can prove to yourself the enormous returns possible in your own life by putting the secret to a practical test.

I want you to make a test that will last 30 days. It is not going to be easy, but if you will give it a good try, it will completely change your life for the better.

Back in the 17th Century, Sir Isaac Newton, the English mathematician and natural philosopher gave us the natural laws of physics, which apply as much to human beings as they do to the movement of bodies in the universe. And one of these laws is: "For every action, there is an equal and opposite reaction".

Simply stated as it applies to you and me, it means we can achieve nothing without paying the price.

The results of your 30-day experiment will be in direct proportion to the effort you put forth. To be a doctor, you must pay the price of long years of difficult study. To be successful in selling, and remember each of us succeeds in life to the extent of our ability to sell,

- selling our families on our ideas,
- selling education in schools,
- selling our children on the advantages of living a good and honest life,
- selling our associates and employees on the importance of being exceptional people.

Too of course, the profession of selling itself.

But to be successful in selling our way of the good life, we must be willing to pay the price. What is that price? Well it is many things.

First, it is understanding emotionally as well as intellectually that we literally become what we think about, that we must control our thoughts if we are to control our lives. It is understanding fully that: "*As ye sow, so shall ye reap.*"

Second, it is cutting away all fetters from the mind and permitting it to soar as it was divinely designed to do. It is the realization that your limitations are self-imposed, and the opportunities for you today are enormous beyond belief. It is rising above narrow-minded pettiness and prejudice.

And third, it is using all your courage to force yourself to think positively on your own problem. To set a definite and clearly defined goal for yourself and to let your marvelous mind think about your goal from all possible angles, to let your imagination speculate freely upon many different possible solutions. To refuse to believe that there are any circumstances sufficiently strong to defeat you in the accomplishment of your purpose. To act promptly and decisively when your course is clear and to keep constantly aware of the fact that you are at this moment standing in the middle of your own "Acres of Diamonds" as Russel Conwell points out in his book.

And fourth, save at least ten cents of every dollar you earn.

It is also remembering that no matter what your present job, it has enormous possibilities, if you are willing to pay the price.

Let's go over the important points in the price each of us must pay to achieve the wonderful life that can be ours.

It is of course worth any price.

One: Think - You will become what you think about.

Two: Imagine - Remember the word imagination and let your mind begin to soar.

Three: Courage - Concentrate on your goal every day.

Four: Save - ten percent of what you earn.

Five: Action - Ideas are worthless unless we act on them.

Next, I'll outline the 30 day test I want you to make, keeping in mind that you have nothing to lose by making this test, and everything you could possibly want to gain.

There are two things that may be said about everyone:

1) Each of us wants something, and

2) Each of us is afraid of something.

For the next 30 days, follow each of these steps every day until you have achieved your goal.

First, write on a card what it is you want more than anything else.

It may be more money. Perhaps you'd like to double your income or make a specific amount of money.

It may be a beautiful home.

It may be success at your job.

It may be a particular position in life.

It could be a more harmonious family.

Each of us wants something.

Write down on your card specifically what it is you want.

Make sure it's a single goal and clearly defined. You need not show it to anyone, in fact often it is best not to. (*Cast not your pearls before swine, lest they trample them, and turn again and rend you.* - Matthew 7)

Carry the card with you so that you can look at it several times a day. Think about your goals in a cheerful, relaxed, positive way each morning when you get up, and immediately you have something to work for - something to get out of bed for, something to live for.

Look at the goals written on your card every chance you get during the day and just before going to bed at night. As you look at it, remember that you must become what you think about, and since you're thinking about your goal, you realize that soon it will be yours.

In fact, it is really yours the moment you write it down and begin to think about it. Look at the abundance all around you as you as you go about your daily business. You have as much right to this abundance as any living creature. It is yours for the asking.

Now we come to the difficult part. Difficult because it means the formation of what is probably a brand-new habit. New habits are not easily formed. Once formed however, they will follow you for the rest of your life.

Second, stop thinking about what it is you fear.

Each time a fearful or negative thought comes into your conscious mind, replace it with a mental picture of your positive and worthwhile goal. And there will come times when you'll feel like giving up. It's easier for a human being to think negatively than positively. That's why only five percent are successful!

You must begin now to place yourself in that group. For 30 days you must take control of your mind. It will think about only what you permit it to think about. Each day for this 30-day test, do more than you have to do.

In addition to maintaining a cheerful positive outlook, give of yourself more than you have ever done before. Do this knowing that your returns in life must be in direct proportion to what you give.

The moment you decide on a goal to work toward, you immediately are a successful person. You are then in that rare and successful category of people who know where they are going. Out of every 100 people, you belong to the top five.

Don't concern yourself too much with how you are going to achieve your goal. Leave that completely to a power greater than yourself. The answers will come to you of their own accord and at the right time. (As

Jiminy Cricket sings: "Like a bolt out of the blue, Fate steps in and sees you through!")

All you have to know is where you are going.

Remember these words from the sermon on the mount, and remember them well. Keep them constantly before you this month of your test.

Ask, And It Shall Be Given You
Seek, And Ye Shall Find
"Knock, And It Shall Be Opened Unto You
For Every One That Asketh Receiveth

It is as marvelous and as simple as that. In fact it is so simple, that in our seemingly complicated world, it is difficult for an adult to understand that all they need is a purpose... and faith.

For 30 days, do your very best.

If you are a salesman, go at it as you have never done before, not in a hectic fashion, but with the calm cheerful assurance that time well spent will give you the abundance in return that you want.

If you are a homemaker, devote your 30-day test to completely giving of yourself without thinking of receiving anything in return, and you will be amazed at the difference it makes in your life.

No matter what your job, do it as you have never done before, and if you have kept your goal before you every day for 30 days, you will wonder and marvel at this new life you have found.

Dorothea Brande, the outstanding editor and writer, discovered it for herself and talks about it in her fine book "Wake up and Live". Her entire philosophy is reduced to the words: "Act as though it were impossible to fail." She made her own test, with sincerity and faith, and her entire life was changed to overwhelming success.

Now, you make your test for 30 full days.

Don't start your test until you have made up your mind to stick with it. You see by being persistent, you are demonstrating faith. Persistence is simply another word for faith. If you did not have faith, you would never persist.

If you should fail within your first 30 days, by that I mean finding yourself overwhelmed by negative thoughts - you have to start over again from that point and go 30 more days.

Gradually, your new habit will form, until you find yourself one of that wonderful minority to whom virtually nothing is impossible.

And don't forget the card.

It is vitally important as you begin this new way of living.

On one side of the card, write your goal, whatever it may be. On the other side, write the words we've quoted from the sermon on the mount.

"Ask, And It Shall Be Given You"

"Seek, And Ye Shall Find"

"Knock, And It Shall Be Opened Unto You"

"For Every One That Asketh Receiveth"

In your spare time during your test period read books that will help you. Read at least 15 minutes each day. Inspirational books like The Bible, Dorothea Brand's "Wake up and Live" if you can still find a copy, "The Magic of Believing" by Claude Bristol, "Think and Grow Rich" by Napoleon Hill, and other books that instruct and inspire.

Nothing great was ever accomplished without inspiration. See that during these crucial first 30 days your own inspiration is kept to a peak.

Above all... don't worry! Worry brings fear, and fear is crippling. The only thing that can cause you to worry during your test is trying to do it all yourself. Know that all you have to do is hold your goal before you; everything else will take care of itself.

Remember also to keep calm and cheerful, don't let petty things annoy you and get you off course.

Now since making this test is difficult, some will say, "Why should I bother?"

Well look at the alternative.

No one wants to be a failure.

No one really wants to be a mediocre individual.

No one wants a life constantly full of fear and worry and frustration.

Therefore, remember that you will reap that which you sow. If you sow negative thoughts, your life will be filled with negative things. If you sow positive thoughts, your life will be cheerful, successful, and positive.

Gradually you will have a tendency to forget what you have just learned. Read this again each week. Keep reminding yourself of what you must do to form this new habit. Gather your whole family around at regular intervals and listen to what has been said here.

Most people will tell you that they want to make money, without understanding the law. The only people who make money work in a mint. The rest of us must earn money.

This is what causes those who keep looking for something for nothing, or a free ride, to fail in life. The only way to earn money is by providing people with services or products which are needed and useful.

We exchange our time and our product or service for the other person's money.

Therefore, the law is that our financial return will be in direct proportion to our service. Success is not the result of making money. Earning money is the result of success - and success is in direct proportion to our service.

Most people have this law backwards. They believe that you are successful if you earn a lot of money. The truth is that you can only earn money after you are successful.

It's like the man who stands in front of the stove and says to it: "Give me heat and then I'll add the wood." How many men and women do you know, or do you suppose there are today, who take the same attitude toward life? There are millions.

We've got to put the fuel in before we can expect heat. Likewise, we've got to be of service first before we can expect money.

Don't concern yourself with the money. Be of service ... build ... work ...dream ...create! Do this and you'll find there is no limit to the prosperity and abundance that will come to you.

Prosperity is founded upon a law of mutual exchange. Any person who contributes to prosperity must prosper in turn themselves.

Sometimes the return will not come from those you serve, but it must come to you from someplace, because that is the law.

For every action, there is an equal and opposite reaction.

As you go daily through your 30-day test period, your success will always be measured by the quality and quantity of service you render, and money is a yardstick for measuring this service. No person can get rich themselves, unless they first enrich others. There are no exceptions to a law.

You can drive down any street and from your car estimate the service that is being rendered by the people living on that street.

Have you ever thought of this yardstick before? It's interesting. Some, like ministers, priests and other devoted people measure their returns in the realm of the spiritual, but again their returns are equal to their service.

Once this law is understood, any thinking person can tell their own fortune. If they want more, they must be of more service to those he receives his return. If they want less, they have only to reduce their service. This is the price you must pay for what you want.

If you believe you can enrich yourself by deluding others, you can end only by deluding yourself. It may take some time, but as surely as you breathe, you will get back what you put out.

Don't ever make the mistake of thinking you can avert this. It's impossible: The prisons and the streets where the lonely walk are filled with people who tried to make new laws just for themselves. We may avoid the laws of men for a while, but there are greater laws that cannot be broken.

An outstanding medical doctor recently pointed out six steps that will help you realize success.

1. Set yourself a definite goal.

2. Quit running yourself down.

3. Stop thinking of all the reasons why you cannot be successful and instead think of all the reasons why you can.

4. Trace your attitudes back through your childhood and discover where you first got the idea that you could not be successful if that is the way you've been thinking.

5. Change the image you have of yourself by writing out a description of the person you would like to be.

6. Act the part of the successful person you have decided to become.

The doctor that wrote those words is a noted west coast psychiatrist, Dr. David Harold Fink.

Do what the experts since the dawn of recorded history have told you you must do: pay the price by becoming the person you want to become. It's not nearly as difficult as living unsuccessfully.

Take this 30-day test, then repeat it ... then repeat it again.

Each time it will become more a part of you until you'll wonder how you could have ever have lived any other way. Live this new way and the floodgates of abundance will open and pour over you more riches than you may have dreamed existed.

Money? Yes, lots of it.

But what's more important, you'll have peace ... you'll be in that wonderful minority who lead calm, cheerful, successful lives.

Start today. You have nothing to lose - but you have your whole life to win.

This is Earl Nightingale . . . Thank you.

Text *of* Video Version

Introduction

Back in 1956, I wrote and recorded something we called the Strangest Secret. Without advertising or fanfare of any kind it outsold all other non-musical, non-entertainment type recordings. It has been heard by millions and millions of people throughout the free world and in the process created a brand-new industry: learning through listening, on one of these solid-state cassette tape players. This player has revolutionized the learning process. Now people listen in their automobiles while they are driving to and from work and on sales calls, time that was formerly wasted, on their commuter train with the little earpiece, in the bathroom while shaving in the morning, or at the dinner table with the children gathered around the table and the whole family together, for a change. This has made a tremendous difference in the business of learning.

But, getting back to the Strangest Secret. What makes it a best seller? What is it about that recording that caused millions and millions of people to want to hear it over and over again and let their children hear it and play it for their employees and sales forces. Well I'm making a talk here today in which I will cover the highlights and philosophy of the Strangest Secret, and I'd like to invite you to join us. I hope you find it of some value.

I want to tell you the most interesting story in the world. Why a person becomes the person they become. Why a little boy or a little girl grows up to be the kind of person he or she becomes.

The estimates by the experts in this field are that most of us are using somewhere around 5% of our real potential, some experts say as little as 1%.

It means that we are only giving about 5% of ourselves to what we are doing, to our days, our work, our families, everyone we know, our entire environment.

But it also means that we are only experiencing 5% of the fun, 5% of the joy, 5% of the rewards we could be knowing, or less.

All the experts are agreed that in each of us, there are deep reservoirs of ability, even genius, that we habitually fail to use.

Why?

We know that most people desire by nature to succeed. But what is success?

What is this word that has become so famous in the world?

What does it mean?

Most people do not know what success is all about, and since they do not know what it is about, they really don't know where to look for it.

Success is really nothing more than the progressive realization of a worthy ideal. This means that any person who knows what they are doing and where they are going is a success. Any person with a goal towards which they are working is a successful person.

This means that a boy in high school working towards a diploma, the girl in college towards a degree, is just as successful as any human being on earth, because they know what they are doing, why they are getting up in the morning, and where they are going.

But conversely, if a person doesn't know what they are working toward, what it is they want, doesn't have a goal towards which they are working, then they, at least by this definition, be called unsuccessful.

Why isn't then, with this simple definition, why isn't everyone successful? It should be easy. Yet surveys indicate that 19 out of 20, 95% at least are not. In fact a survey one time asked thousands of working men why they got up in the morning and went to work, and 19 out of 20 didn't know.

19 out of 20 working people didn't have the foggiest notion why they got up in the morning and went to work. Under closer questioning they said, "Well, everyone works."

Well, that would be a good reason to quit. In fact, a little rule of thumb you might want to remember: Whatever the great majority is doing under any given circumstance, if you do exactly the opposite, you will probably never make another mistake as long as you live. Just something to keep in the back of your mind.

The problem with most people is that they are playing the world's most unrewarding game, and the name of the game is: Follow the Follower.

There is a story about a small town in which there was a jewelry store, and like all jewelry stores, or most jewelry stores at least, there was a big clock in their front window.

Every morning for years, the jeweler had noticed a working man stop, adjust his pocket watch to the same time as the clock in the window.

He has been doing this for many years. One morning the jeweler was out in front sweeping his sidewalk, and asked the man, "Why do you adjust your watch to my big clock every morning? I've noticed you doing that for years." The man said, "Well I'm the foreman down at the big plant. I want to make sure my watch is correct because I blow the quitting whistle every night at 5 o'clock.

The jeweler looked at him rather strangely for a moment, and then he said, "Well that's funny, I've been setting that big clock in the window by that quitting whistle all these years."

A very logical thing, but between them they could have been off six months! It is a case of people just going along with what they thought to be correct without checking their references.

So I want to suggest that from now on out, at least we do that. That we check our references, and ask ourselves, "Are the people I'm following going where I want to go?"

Let me tell you the story of what we might call the average young man in our society. From the time this boy is born, there is only one thing on this earth he can do, and that is to begin to think, act, and talk like the people by whom he is surrounded. This is all in the world he can do.

But right off the bat, the odds are 95 to 5 that he is thinking, acting, and talking like the wrong group. They are wonderful people, they love him, they would do anything in the world for him, they want him to succeed, but the odds are 95 to 5 that they have not got the answers he needs if he is to reach fulfillment as a human being, if he is to reach this success that he wants, if he is to reach into the deep reservoirs of ability and genius, we know he possesses and draw it out.

Well, he starts in school. The most important thing to a boy in school is to be liked by the other little boys in school. And so at this tender age he begins to follow other little boys his same age, who don't know any more than he knows, do not have his best interests at heart, and who do not necessarily have any capacity for leadership.

He does this in the first grade, and the second, and the third, and the fourth, and the fifth, and the sixth, and the seventh, and the eighth, and year after year after year he forms himself into a composite average of other little boys his age, trying to be like them. Trying to do the only thing in the world it is impossible for a human being to do, which is to be like somebody else.

Now let's say he goes all the way through school, and then usually he goes in the military service. Again, he is caught in the viselike grip of conformity.

Now let's say he is 25 years old, out of school, out of the service. What's he going to do? As a rule, he will go back to his home town, unless he is married in which case he will go to his wife's home town, but let's say he goes back to his own home town.

He is single. He doesn't know quite what to do. He is standing on a corner one morning and a friend that he knew in school comes up and says, "Hi there Charlie! What are you doing?"

He says, "Nothing." His friend says, "Why don't you come down and work where I work. It's a pretty good place, the pay is regular, we've got all kinds of fringe benefits... and so on." And so he does.

The odds are about again 95 to 5 that his first job is taken as a result of random application.

On the job, without thinking about it, the most natural thing in the world for him to do is to look around, see how the other guys are doing their job, and begin doing his the same way, assuming that what is normal for them is normal for him. No reason for this, he doesn't think about it, he just does it.

Now he has stretching in front of him fifty years or more in the golden age that man has been dreaming of since the days of ancient Greece. What is he going to do with these fifty golden years? Well let's take a good close look at him. We know that he works 40 hours a week, as a rule. This leaves him 72 hours a week when he is neither working nor sleeping. 72 free discretionary hours each week to do with as he pleases.

Now at this point of course he is married and has his little house and little car. And this is about what he does with his free 72 hours every week. He'll do what the other guys are doing with their free 72 hours every week, which is virtually nothing at all.

On a typical day, he'll quit right on the dot, get in his little car, go to his little house, go in his little kitchen, kiss his little wife, and say I'm tired. They have even figured out why he says that. The experts believe that he used to hear his father say that back when men used to get tired working during the day and he picked it up and he repeats this every night when he gets home.

He bolts down his little meal and then he heads to the living room where he turns on his escape box. Click!

It takes 15-20 seconds for the screen to light up, a period of time he finds interminable, but he gets through it somehow, kicks the dog or thumbs through a magazine or something.

Then the screen lights up and he does too a little bit. There in front of him he sees people in all kinds of funny old-time costumes all killing each other at a great rate. Now one expert has agreed that the average family can see more death and bloodshed and carnage on the television set in a week than Crassus saw when he crucified 6000 prisoners on the southern road to Rome, but you know how those experts are, they can certainly be off one or two.

But he sits there for five or six hours. Twenty five percent of all free time now is spent in front of the tube according to the latest statistics.

Now there is nothing wrong with this particularly, except that he is watching other people who are earning excellent incomes in the pursuit of their careers while he does not make a nickel, and gets one of the only two things you can get by watching TV on that kind of a schedule... red eyes and a hollow head.

This is not meant to be an indictment of television I've got a couple of television sets at home too. I've got a couple of cars at home too, but I don't go home at night and drive around the block for six hours! If there is someplace I want to go, fine, my car will take me there. If there is a great program, like a golf match or something like that, I want to see it.

But he sits there for five or six hours until finally his wife, who is a little more practical than him, taps him on the shoulder and says, "Charlie, I think it is about time you went to bed. You've got to get up in the morning and go to work." He says OK and shuts it off, he knows how to do that, he just shuts it off and goes to bed.

The next morning, he gets up and he does this all over again. He does this every day for 40 years. At the end of 40 years he gets retired, which always kind of catches him by surprise, no one has ever figured that out either, and then he dies at 85 or 90, the way medical science is moving us along, out of sheer boredom.

Well, what is the problem? Is there a tragedy here? Not really if that is the way Charlie, our mythical, hypothetical young man, wants to spend his life. If he wants to spend his life that way, that is his business. He lives in a free society. He can do anything with his life that he wants.

But there is a terrible tragedy here if he is living that way because of a total lack of a decision. If he is living that way simply because he is still doing what he was doing in the first and second grade, and that is going along with all the fellows up and down the block on the unspoken assumption that they know how to live. Then there is a real tragedy there, because they have never known how to live, not in all the recorded history of mankind.

He never finds out who he is. He never reaches into the deep depths of his abilities, his talents. He never learns that he can have just about everything he wants in the world, that he can call his own shots, tell his own fortune. And it's kind of a pity.

Well, what is new? What is needed, I think, is a checklist like an airplane pilot uses. I think that living successfully is at least as important as flying an airplane. Here are some of the things that, I think, should be on that checklist, that could help this young man live a more interesting, more meaningful, more exciting, more enjoyable life.

The first thing that he ought to have on his checklist, in my opinion, is the word: "Goal". A man without a goal is like a ship without a rudder. He doesn't know where he is going. He then belongs to that 95% that are just living day by day, week after week, month after month like a starfish or an amoeba. He needs to know where he is going.

Back in the early days of navigation, sailors used to see a strange sight in the Antarctic. They used to see a giant iceberg towering high out of the sea, and it would be moving against the wind. The wind would be blowing one way and the iceberg would be moving right into the teeth of the wind. This frightened the sailors whose ships were powered by the wind, until it was discovered that only a fraction of the great iceberg was visible and its huge ponderous roots were caught in the great currents of the ocean. It was being carried purposely along its way regardless of the winds and the tides on the surface. This is what a man needs.

He needs his roots deep in the great mainstream of his own choosing, and then he'll move along his way regardless of the winds on the surface of his life or short-term expediency. And then he will get to where he is going.

A second word on our checklist might be the word: "Attitude". It has been called the most important word in any language in the world, because it is our attitude toward our world and toward all the people in it that will determine the world's attitude and all the people's attitude toward us. It is a simple thing, most of us know it but we tend to forget it. People will react to us according to our attitude. Our attitude is the greatest gift we can be given.

You know, the little creatures of the world were given a wonderful gift by Mother Nature called protective coloring which lets them blend into their background so they cannot be seen. But man was not given this great gift, because man was given an incalculably greater one. Only man has the godlike power to make his surroundings change to fit him, because his environment will change as he changes. A man's environment is a merciless mirror of him as a human being. If he thinks his environment could stand a little improvement, all he has to do is improve and his environment will improve to reflect the change in him.

Third would be the word: "Think". To think, the highest function of which a human being is capable. It was put pretty well by the great Pulitzer Prize winning playwright Archibald McLeish[1] in his great play "The Secret of Freedom" in which he has one of his characters saying, "The only thing about a man that is a man... is his mind. Everything else you can find in a pig or a horse." It's true!

And so if we are going to develop something, this is a good place to start. To think deliberately, and with a purpose. To spend a little time each day before a blank sheet of paper with our goal perhaps written at the top. To come up with some fresh new exciting ideas.

Our checklist should include what you might call the law of laws. That's what Emerson called it. The great old law of cause and effect. That our rewards in life will always be in exact proportion to our contribution to our service. We all know this really. We tell our children in Sunday School, "*As Ye sow So Shall Ye Reap*", but we forget that that is true. If a man is unhappy with his rewards, all in the world that his has to do is find ways of increasing his contribution, his service.

It reminds me of the story of the preacher who was driving down a country road when he came upon the most magnificent farm he had ever seen in his life. It was beautiful. He saw the farmer approaching the road on his tractor, so he hailed him. "My good man, God has certainly blessed you with a magnificent farm." The farmer thought for a moment and replied, "Yes, you are right, he certainly has. But you should have seen this place when he had it all to himself." The preacher had his sermon for the next Sunday. He realized that all the farmers up and down that road had been given the same land, yet one man had made something great out of it.

Well all of us have been given the same land. We are given a human life, and each of us can make something great out of it too if we want.

---

[1] *American poet, writer, and the Librarian of Congress. He is associated with the Modernist school of poetry. He received three Pulitzer Prizes for his work.*

The next point might be simply the word: "Truth." Since everything we do has an equal and opposite reaction, unless what we are doing is based on truth, we are building on sand, and it can't stand.

Next would be: R&D, research and development. None of us would want to work for a company, or invest our money in a company that did not have a very viable research and development department, that is pumping a good percentage of its profits back into research and development because its future depends on it. And so does a man's future depend on it.

You might ask yourself how much of your take home pay and discretionary time have you spent during the past year on materials calculated to make you smarter this year than you were the year before. Calculated to make you a little better, a little bigger as a human being. To perhaps love a little more, hate a little less, do a little better job than you did a year ago. How much time and money are you pumping back into yourself and your future? It's worth thinking about.

And finally, the Strangest Secret. At the beginning I asked, "What makes a child grow up to be the human being he becomes?" Well, this is the reason for that.

Of course, he is the confluence of a genetic pool that goes back for thousands and thousands of years. And his environment has an influence on him of course. But what makes him the person he becomes is that **he becomes what he thinks about most of the time**. It is as simple as that. We become what we think about most of the time. And that is the Strangest Secret.

This is why thinking is so vital. This is why a goal is so important. Because we will become that. This is why people who set goals achieve them. The trouble with men is not in achieving their goals, they do that. It is in establishing them.

Well that is about it. I think it is good to remember, if we just go along with the crowd, we won't wind up with much more than the wish that we could do it all over again, and as far as we know you can't. If we want to amount to anything as individuals, we need: individual goals, individual thinking, individual actions, and we must never conform to the big group. We must love them, We must help them, We must serve them because our entire success will depend on our ability to do these things, but never lose our individuality and our identity by permitting ourselves to become submerged in what has historically proved itself to be little more than a suffocating sea of indirection and purposelessness. If we want to emulate someone, fine, but let's be choosy in whose steps we follow. It's the only life we've got. And remember to think. Imagination is everything, and we can become what we can imagine.

If you find yourself getting depressed and down at the mouth, as we all get once in a while, you might want to remember this quotation by Dean Briggs. He said, "Do your work. Not just your work and no more, but a little more for the lavishing sake, that little more which is worth all the rest. And if you suffer as you must and you doubt as you must, do your work. Put your heart into it and the sky will clear. And then out of your very doubt and suffering will be born the supreme joy of life. Believe it or not, in an age where we've come to nearly deify leisure time, we have virtually lost sight of the fact that nearly all our satisfactions and rewards will come, not from our leisure, but from our work.

And don't forget "The Strangest Secret".

We become what we think about.

As A Man Thinketh

Authorized Edition

James Allen

Mind is the Master power that molds and makes,
And Man is Mind, and evermore he takes
The tool of Thought, and, shaping what he wills,
Brings forth a thousand joys, a thousand ills:
He thinks in secret, and it comes to pass:
Environment is but his looking-glass.

Contents

Foreword

This little volume (the result of meditation and experience) is not intended as an exhaustive treatise on the much-written-upon subject of the power of thought. It is suggestive rather than explanatory, its object being to stimulate men and women to the discovery and perception of the truth that:

"They themselves are makers of themselves,"

by virtue of the thoughts, which they choose and encourage; that mind is the master-weaver, both of the inner garment of character and the outer garment of circumstance, and that, as they may have hitherto woven in ignorance and pain they may now weave in enlightenment and happiness.

James Allen

Broad Park Avenue,
Ilfracombe,
England

Thought & Character

The aphorism, "As a man thinketh in his heart so is he," not only embraces the whole of a man's being, but is so comprehensive as to reach out to every condition and circumstance of his life. A man is literally *what he thinks*, his character being the complete sum of all his thoughts.

As the plant springs from, and could not be without, the seed, so every act of a man springs from the hidden seeds of thought, and could not have appeared without them. This applies equally to those acts called "spontaneous" and "unpremeditated" as to those, which are deliberately executed.

Act is the blossom of thought, and joy and suffering are its fruits; thus does a man garner in the sweet and bitter fruitage of his own husbandry.

> "Thought in the mind hath made us, What we are
> By thought was wrought and built. If a man's mind
> Hath evil thoughts, pain comes on him as comes
> The wheel the ox behind . . .
>
> . . . If one endure
> In purity of thought, joy follows him
> As his own shadow—sure."

Man is a growth by law, and not a creation by artifice, and cause and effect are as absolute and undeviating in the hidden realm of thought as in the world of visible and material things. A noble and Godlike character is not a thing of favor or chance, but is the natural result of continued effort in right thinking, the effect of long-cherished association with Godlike thoughts. An ignoble and bestial character, by the same process, is the result of the continued harboring of groveling thoughts.

Man is made or unmade by himself; in the armory of thought he forges the weapons by which he destroys himself; he also fashions the tools with which he builds for himself heavenly mansions of joy and strength and peace. By the right choice and true application of thought, man ascends to the Divine Perfection; by the abuse and wrong application of thought, he descends below the level of the beast. Between these two extremes are all the grades of character, and man is their maker and master.

Of all the beautiful truths pertaining to the soul which have been restored and brought to light in this age, none is more gladdening or fruitful of divine promise and confidence than this—that man is the master of thought, the molder of character, and the maker and shaper of condition, environment, and destiny.

As a being of Power, Intelligence, and Love, and the lord of his own thoughts, man holds the key to every situation, and contains within himself that transforming and regenerative agency by which he may make himself what he wills.

Man is always the master, even in his weaker and most abandoned state; but in his weakness and degradation he is the foolish master who misgoverns his "household." When he begins to reflect upon his condition, and to search diligently for the Law upon which his being is established, he then becomes the wise master, directing his energies with intelligence, and fashioning his thoughts to fruitful issues. Such is the *conscious* master, and man can only thus become by discovering *within himself* the laws of thought; which discovery is totally a matter of application, self-analysis, and experience.

Only by much searching and mining, are gold and diamonds obtained, and man can find every truth connected with his being, if he will dig deep into the mine of his soul; and that he is the maker of his character, the molder of his life, and the builder of his destiny, he may unerringly prove, if he will watch, control, and alter his thoughts, tracing their effects upon himself, upon others, and upon his life and circumstances, linking cause and effect by patient practice and investigation, and utilizing his every experience, even to the most trivial, everyday occurrence, as a means of obtaining that knowledge of himself which is Understanding, Wisdom, Power. In this direction, as in no other, is the law absolute that "He that seeketh findeth; and to him that knocketh it shall be opened;" for only by patience, practice, and ceaseless importunity can a man enter the Door of the Temple of Knowledge.

Effect *of* Thought
on Circumstances

Man's mind may be likened to a garden, which may be intelligently cultivated or allowed to run wild; but whether cultivated or neglected, it must, and will, *bring forth*. If no useful seeds are *put* into it, then an abundance of useless weed-seeds will *fall* therein, and will continue to produce their kind.

Just as a gardener cultivates his plot, keeping it free from weeds, and growing the flowers and fruits which he requires, so may a man tend the garden of his mind, weeding out all the wrong, useless, and impure thoughts, and cultivating toward perfection the flowers and fruits of right, useful, and pure thoughts. By pursuing this process, a man sooner or later discovers that he is the master-gardener of his soul, the director of his life. He also reveals, within himself, the laws of thought, and understands, with ever-increasing accuracy, how the thought-forces and mind elements operate in the shaping of his character, circumstances, and destiny.

Thought and character are one, and as character can only manifest and discover itself through environment and circumstance, the outer conditions of a person's life will always be found to be harmoniously related to his inner state. This does not mean that a man's circumstances at any given time are an indication of his *entire* character, but that those circumstances are so intimately connected with some vital thought-element within himself that, for the time being, they are indispensable to his development.

Every man is where he is by the law of his being; the thoughts which he has built into his character have brought him there, and in the arrangement of his life there is no element of chance, but all is the result of a law which cannot err. This is just as true of those who feel "out of harmony" with their surroundings as of those who are contented with them.

As a progressive and evolving being, man is where he is that he may learn that he may grow; and as he learns the spiritual lesson which any circumstance contains for him, it passes away and gives place to other circumstances.

Man is buffeted by circumstances so long as he believes himself to be the creature of outside conditions, but when he realizes that he is a creative power, and that he may command the hidden soil and seeds of his being out of which circumstances grow, he then becomes the rightful master of himself.

That circumstances grow out of thought every man knows who has for any length of time practiced self-control and self-purification, for he will have noticed that the alteration in his circumstances has been in exact ratio with his altered mental condition. So true is this that when a man earnestly applies himself to remedy the defects in his character, and makes swift and marked progress, he passes rapidly through a succession of vicissitudes.

The soul attracts that which it secretly harbors; that which it loves, and also that which it fears; it reaches the height of its cherished aspirations; it falls to the level of its unchastened desires, and circumstances are the means by which the soul receives its own.

Every thought-seed sown or allowed to fall into the mind, and to take root there, produces its own, blossoming sooner or later into act, and bearing its own fruitage of opportunity and circumstance. Good thoughts bear good fruit, bad thoughts bad fruit.

The outer world of circumstance shapes itself to the inner world of thought, and both pleasant and unpleasant external conditions are factors, which make for the ultimate good of the individual. As the reaper of his own harvest, man learns both by suffering and bliss.

Following the inmost desires, aspirations, thoughts, by which he allows himself to be dominated, (pursuing the will-o'-the-wisps of impure imaginings or steadfastly walking the highway of strong and high endeavor), a man at last arrives at their fruition and fulfilment in the outer conditions of his life. The laws of growth and adjustment everywhere obtains.

A man does not come to the almshouse or the jail by the tyranny of fate or circumstance, but by the pathway of groveling thoughts and base desires. Nor does a pure-minded man fall suddenly into crime by stress of any mere external force; the criminal thought had long been secretly fostered in the heart, and the hour of opportunity revealed its gathered power. Circumstance does not make the man; it reveals him to himself No such conditions can exist as descending into vice and its attendant sufferings apart from vicious inclinations, or ascending into virtue and its pure happiness without the continued cultivation of virtuous aspirations; and man, therefore, as the lord and master of thought, is the maker of himself the shaper and author of environment.

Even at birth the soul comes to its own and through every step of its earthly pilgrimage it attracts those combinations of conditions which reveal itself, which are the reflections of its own purity and, impurity, its strength and weakness.

Men do not attract that which they *want*, but that which they *are*. Their whims, fancies, and ambitions are thwarted at every step, but their inmost thoughts and desires are fed with their own food, be it foul or clean. The "divinity that shapes our ends" is in ourselves; it is our very self. Only himself manacles man: thought and action are the jailers of Fate—they imprison, being base; they are also the angels of Freedom—they liberate, being noble. Not what he wishes and prays for does a man get, but what he justly earns. His wishes and prayers are only gratified and answered when they harmonize with his thoughts and actions.

In the light of this truth, what, then, is the meaning of "fighting against circumstances?" It means that a man is continually revolting against an *effect* without, while all the time he is nourishing and preserving its *cause* in his heart. That cause may take the form of a conscious vice or an unconscious weakness; but whatever it is, it stubbornly retards the efforts of its possessor, and thus calls aloud for remedy.

Men are anxious to improve their circumstances, but are unwilling to improve themselves; they therefore remain bound. The man who does not shrink from self-crucifixion can never fail to accomplish the object upon which his heart is set. This is as true of earthly as of heavenly things. Even the man whose sole object is to acquire wealth must be prepared to make great personal sacrifices before he can accomplish his object; and how much more so he who would realize a strong and well-poised life?

Here is a man who is wretchedly poor. He is extremely anxious that his surroundings and home comforts should be improved, yet all the time he shirks his work, and considers he is justified in trying to deceive his employer on the ground of the insufficiency of his wages. Such a man does not understand the simplest rudiments of those principles which are the basis of true prosperity, and is not only totally unfitted to rise out of his wretchedness, but is actually attracting to himself a still deeper wretchedness by dwelling in, and acting out, indolent, deceptive, and unmanly thoughts.

Here is a rich man who is the victim of a painful and persistent disease as the result of gluttony. He is willing to give large sums of money to get rid of it, but he will not sacrifice his gluttonous desires.

He wants to gratify his taste for rich and unnatural viands and have his health as well. Such a man is totally unfit to have health, because he has not yet learned the first principles of a healthy life.

Here is an employer of labor who adopts crooked measures to avoid paying the regulation wage, and, in the hope of making larger profits, reduces the wages of his workpeople. Such a man is altogether unfitted for prosperity, and when he finds himself bankrupt, both as regards reputation and riches, he blames circumstances, not knowing that he is the sole author of his condition.

I have introduced these three cases merely as illustrative of the truth that man is the causer (though nearly always is unconsciously) of his circumstances, and that, whilst aiming at a good end, he is continually frustrating its accomplishment by encouraging thoughts and desires which cannot possibly harmonize with that end. Such cases could be multiplied and varied almost indefinitely, but this is not necessary, as the reader can, if he so resolves, trace the action of the laws of thought in his own mind and life, and until this is done, mere external facts cannot serve as a ground of reasoning.

Circumstances, however, are so complicated, thought is so deeply rooted, and the conditions of happiness vary so, vastly with individuals, that a man's entire soul-condition (although it may be known to himself) cannot be judged by another from the external aspect of his life alone. A man may be honest in certain directions, yet suffer privations; a man may be dishonest in certain directions, yet acquire wealth; but the conclusion usually formed that the one man fails *because of his particular honesty*, and that the other *prospers because of his particular dishonesty*, is the result of a superficial judgment, which assumes that the dishonest man is almost totally corrupt, and the honest man almost entirely virtuous. In the light of a deeper knowledge and wider experience such judgment is found to be erroneous. The dishonest man may have some admirable virtues, which the other does, not possess; and the honest man obnoxious vices which are absent in the other. The honest man reaps the good results of his honest thoughts and acts; he also brings upon himself the sufferings, which his vices produce. The dishonest man likewise garners his own suffering and happiness.

It is pleasing to human vanity to believe that one suffers because of one's virtue; but not until a man has extirpated every sickly, bitter, and impure thought from his mind, and washed every sinful stain from his soul, can he be in a position to know and declare that his sufferings are the result of his good, and not of his bad qualities; and on the way to, yet long before he has reached, that supreme perfection, he will have found, working in his mind and life, the Great Law which is absolutely just, and which cannot, therefore, give good for evil, evil for good. Possessed of such knowledge, he will then know, looking back upon his past ignorance and blindness, that his life is, and always was, justly ordered, and that all his past experiences, good and bad, were the equitable outworking of his evolving, yet unevolved self.

Good thoughts and actions can never produce bad results; bad thoughts and actions can never produce good results. This is but saying that nothing can come from corn but corn, nothing from nettles but nettles. Men understand this law in the natural world, and work with it; but few understand it in the mental and moral world (though its operation there is just as simple and undeviating), and they, therefore, do not co-operate with it.

Suffering is *always* the effect of wrong thought in some direction. It is an indication that the individual is out of harmony with himself, with the Law of his being. The sole and supreme use of suffering is to purify, to burn out all that is useless and impure. Suffering ceases for him who is pure. There could be no object in burning gold after the dross had been removed, and a perfectly pure and enlightened being could not suffer.

The circumstances, which a man encounters with suffering, are the result of his own mental in harmony. The circumstances, which a man encounters with blessedness, are the result of his own mental harmony. Blessedness, not material possessions, is the measure of right thought; wretchedness, not lack of material possessions, is the measure of wrong thought. A man may be cursed and rich; he may be blessed and poor. Blessedness and riches are only joined together when the riches are rightly and wisely used; and the poor man only descends into wretchedness when he regards his lot as a burden unjustly imposed.

Indigence and indulgence are the two extremes of wretchedness. They are both equally unnatural and the result of mental disorder. A man is not rightly conditioned until he is a happy, healthy, and prosperous being; and happiness, health, and prosperity are the result of a harmonious adjustment of the inner with the outer, of the man with his surroundings.

A man only begins to be a man when he ceases to whine and revile, and commences to search for the hidden justice which regulates his life. And as he adapts his mind to that regulating factor, he ceases to accuse others as the cause of his condition, and builds himself up in strong and noble thoughts; ceases to kick against circumstances, but begins to *use* them as aids to his more rapid progress, and as a means of discovering the hidden powers and possibilities within himself.

Law, not confusion, is the dominating principle in the universe; justice, not injustice, is the soul and substance of life; and righteousness, not corruption, is the molding and moving force in the spiritual government of the world. This being so, man has but to right himself to find that the universe is right; and during the process of putting himself right he will find that as he alters his thoughts towards things and other people, things and other people will alter towards him.

The proof of this truth is in every person, and it therefore admits of easy investigation by systematic introspection and self-analysis. Let a man radically alter his thoughts, and he will be astonished at the rapid transformation it will affect in the material conditions of his life. Men imagine that thought can be kept secret, but it cannot; it rapidly crystallizes into habit, and habit solidifies into circumstance. Bestial thoughts crystallize into habits of drunkenness and sensuality, which solidify into circumstances of destitution and disease: impure thoughts of every kind crystallize into enervating and confusing habits, which solidify into distracting and adverse circumstances: thoughts of fear, doubt, and indecision crystallize into weak, unmanly, and irresolute habits, which solidify into circumstances of failure, indigence, and slavish dependence: lazy thoughts crystallize into habits of uncleanliness and dishonesty, which solidify into circumstances of foulness and beggary: hateful and condemnatory thoughts crystallize into habits of accusation and violence, which solidify into circumstances of injury and persecution: selfish thoughts of all kinds crystallize into habits of self-seeking, which solidify into circumstances more or less distressing.

On the other hand, beautiful thoughts of all kinds crystallize into habits of grace and kindliness, which solidify into genial and sunny circumstances: pure thoughts crystallize into habits of temperance and self-control, which solidify into circumstances of repose and peace: thoughts of courage, self-reliance, and decision crystallize into manly habits, which solidify into circumstances of success, plenty, and freedom: energetic thoughts crystallize into habits of cleanliness and industry, which solidify into circumstances of pleasantness: gentle and forgiving thoughts crystallize into habits of gentleness, which solidify into protective and preservative circumstances: loving and unselfish thoughts crystallize into habits of self-forgetfulness for others, which solidify into circumstances of sure and abiding prosperity and true riches.

A particular train of thought persisted in, be it good or bad, cannot fail to produce its results on the character and circumstances. A man cannot *directly* choose his circumstances, but he can choose his thoughts, and so indirectly, yet surely, shape his circumstances.

Nature helps every man to the gratification of the thoughts, which he most encourages, and opportunities are presented which will most speedily bring to the surface both the good and evil thoughts.

Let a man cease from his sinful thoughts, and all the world will soften towards him, and be ready to help him; let him put away his weakly and sickly thoughts, and lo, opportunities will spring up on every hand to aid his strong resolves; let him encourage good thoughts, and no hard fate shall bind him down to wretchedness and shame. The world is your kaleidoscope, and the varying combinations of colors, which at every succeeding moment it presents to you are the exquisitely adjusted pictures of your ever-moving thoughts.

> *"So You will be what you will to be;*
> *Let failure find its false content*
> *In that poor word, 'environment,'*
> *But spirit scorns it, and is free.*
>
> *"It masters time, it conquers space;*
> *It cowes that boastful trickster, Chance,*
> *And bids the tyrant Circumstance*
> *Uncrown, and fill a servant's place.*
>
> *"The human Will, that force unseen,*
> *The offspring of a deathless Soul,*
> *Can hew a way to any goal,*
> *Though walls of granite intervene.*
>
> *"Be not impatient in delays*
> *But wait as one who understands;*
> *When spirit rises and commands*
> *The gods are ready to obey."*

Effect *of* Thought *on* Health & *the* Body

The body is the servant of the mind. It obeys the operations of the mind, whether they be deliberately chosen or automatically expressed. At the bidding of unlawful thoughts, the body sinks rapidly into disease and decay; at the command of glad and beautiful thoughts it becomes clothed with youthfulness and beauty.

Disease and health, like circumstances, are rooted in thought. Sickly thoughts will express themselves through a sickly body. Thoughts of fear have been known to kill a man as speedily as a bullet, and they are continually killing thousands of people just as surely though less rapidly. The people who live in fear of disease are the people who get it. Anxiety quickly demoralizes the whole body, and lays it open to the entrance of disease; while impure thoughts, even if not physically indulged, will soon shatter the nervous system.

Strong, pure, and happy thoughts build up the body in vigor and grace. The body is a delicate and plastic instrument, which responds readily to the thoughts by which it is impressed, and habits of thought will produce their own effects, good or bad, upon it.

Men will continue to have impure and poisoned blood, so long as they propagate unclean thoughts. Out of a clean heart comes a clean life and a clean body. Out of a defiled mind proceeds a defiled life and a corrupt body. Thought is the fount of action, life, and manifestation; make the fountain pure, and all will be pure.

Change of diet will not help a man who will not change his thoughts. When a man makes his thoughts pure, he no longer desires impure food.

Clean thoughts make clean habits. The so-called saint who does not wash his body is not a saint. He who has strengthened and purified his thoughts does not need to consider the malevolent microbe.

If you would protect your body, guard your mind. If you would renew your body, beautify your mind. Thoughts of malice, envy, disappointment, despondency, rob the body of its health and grace. A sour face does not come by chance; it is made by sour thoughts. Wrinkles that mar are drawn by folly, passion, and pride.

I know a woman of ninety-six who has the bright, innocent face of a girl. I know a man well under middle age whose face is drawn into inharmonious contours. The one is the result of a sweet and sunny disposition; the other is the outcome of passion and discontent.

As you cannot have a sweet and wholesome abode unless you admit the air and sunshine freely into your rooms, so a strong body and a bright, happy, or serene countenance can only result from the free admittance into the mind of thoughts of joy and goodwill and serenity.

On the faces of the aged there are wrinkles made by sympathy, others by strong and pure thought, and others are carved by passion: who cannot distinguish them? With those who have lived righteously, age is calm, peaceful, and softly mellowed, like the setting sun. I have recently seen a philosopher on his deathbed. He was not old except in years. He died as sweetly and peacefully as he had lived.

There is no physician like cheerful thought for dissipating the ills of the body; there is no comforter to compare with goodwill for dispersing the shadows of grief and sorrow. To live continually in thoughts of ill will, cynicism, suspicion, and envy, is to be confined in a self-made prison-hole. But to think well of all, to be cheerful with all, to patiently learn to find the good in all—such unselfish thoughts are the very portals of heaven; and to dwell day by day in thoughts of peace toward every creature will bring abounding peace to their possessor.

Thought & Purpose

Until thought is linked with purpose there is no intelligent accomplishment. With the majority the bark of thought is allowed to "drift" upon the ocean of life. Aimlessness is a vice, and such drifting must not continue for him who would steer clear of catastrophe and destruction.

They who have no central purpose in their life fall an easy prey to petty worries, fears, troubles, and self-pitying, all of which are indications of weakness, which lead, just as surely as deliberately planned sins (though by a different route), to failure, unhappiness, and loss, for weakness cannot persist in a power evolving universe.

A man should conceive of a legitimate purpose in his heart, and set out to accomplish it. He should make this purpose the centralizing point of his thoughts. It may take the form of a spiritual ideal, or it may be a worldly object, according to his nature at the time being; but whichever it is, he should steadily focus his thought-forces upon the object, which he has set before him. He should make this purpose his supreme duty, and should devote himself to its attainment, not allowing his thoughts to wander away into ephemeral fancies, longings, and imaginings. This is the royal road to self-control and true concentration of thought. Even if he fails again and again to accomplish his purpose (as he necessarily must until weakness is overcome), the *strength of character gained* will be the measure of *his true* success, and this will form a new starting-point for future power and triumph.

Those who are not prepared for the apprehension of a *great* purpose should fix the thoughts upon the faultless performance of their duty, no matter how insignificant their task may appear. Only in this way can the thoughts be gathered and focused, and resolution and energy be developed, which being done, there is nothing which may not be accomplished.

The weakest soul, knowing its own weakness, and believing this truth *that strength can only be developed by effort and practice*, will, thus believing, at once begin to exert itself, and, adding effort to effort, patience to patience, and strength to strength, will never cease to develop, and will at last grow divinely strong.

As the physically weak man can make himself strong by careful and patient training, so the man of weak thoughts can make them strong by exercising himself in right thinking.

To put away aimlessness and weakness, and to begin to think with purpose, is to enter the ranks of those strong ones who only recognize failure as one of the pathways to attainment; who make all conditions serve them, and who think strongly, attempt fearlessly, and accomplish masterfully.

Having conceived of his purpose, a man should mentally mark out a *straight* pathway to its achievement, looking neither to the right nor the left. Doubts and fears should be rigorously excluded; they are disintegrating elements, which break up the straight line of effort, rendering it crooked, ineffectual, useless. Thoughts of doubt and fear never accomplished anything, and never can. They always lead to failure. Purpose, energy, power to do, and all strong thoughts cease when doubt and fear creep in.

The will to do springs from the knowledge that we *can* do. Doubt and fear are the great enemies of knowledge, and he who encourages them, who does not slay them, thwarts himself at every step.

He who has conquered doubt and fear has conquered failure. His every thought is allied with power, and all difficulties are bravely met and wisely overcome. His purposes are seasonably planted, and they bloom and bring forth fruit, which does not fall prematurely to the ground.

Thought allied fearlessly to purpose becomes creative force: he who *knows* this is ready to become something higher and stronger than a mere bundle of wavering thoughts and fluctuating sensations; he who *does* this has become the conscious and intelligent wielder of his mental powers.

The Thought-Factor
in Achievement

All that a man achieves and all that he fails to achieve is the direct result of his own thoughts. In a justly ordered universe, where loss of equipoise would mean total destruction, individual responsibility must be absolute. A man's weakness and strength, purity and impurity, are his own, and not another man's; they are brought about by himself, and not by another; and they can only be altered by himself, never by another. His condition is also his own, and not another man's. His suffering and his happiness are evolved from within. As he thinks, so he is; as he continues to think, so he remains.

A strong man cannot help a weaker unless that weaker is *willing* to be helped, and even then the weak man must become strong of himself; he must, by his own efforts, develop the strength which he admires in another. None but himself can alter his condition.

It has been usual for men to think and to say, "Many men are slaves because one is an oppressor; let us hate the oppressor." Now, however, there is amongst an increasing few a tendency to reverse this judgment, and to say, "One man is an oppressor because many are slaves; let us despise the slaves."

The truth is that oppressor and slave are co-operators in ignorance, and, while seeming to afflict each other, are in reality afflicting themselves. A perfect Knowledge perceives the action of law in the weakness of the oppressed and the misapplied power of the oppressor; a perfect Love, seeing the suffering, which both states entail, condemns neither; a perfect Compassion embraces both oppressor and oppressed.

He who has conquered weakness, and has put away all selfish thoughts, belongs neither to oppressor nor oppressed. He is free.

A man can only rise, conquer, and achieve by lifting up his thoughts. He can only remain weak, and abject, and miserable by refusing to lift up his thoughts.

Before a man can achieve anything, even in worldly things, he must lift his thoughts above slavish animal indulgence. He may not, in order to succeed, give up all animality and selfishness, by any means; but a portion of it must, at least, be sacrificed. A man whose first thought is bestial indulgence could neither think clearly nor plan methodically; he could not find and develop his latent resources, and would fail in any undertaking. Not having commenced to manfully control his thoughts, he is not in a position to control affairs and to adopt serious responsibilities. He is not fit to act independently and stand alone. But he is limited only by the thoughts, which he chooses.

There can be no progress, no achievement without sacrifice, and a man's worldly success will be in the measure that he sacrifices his confused animal thoughts, and fixes his mind on the development of his plans, and the strengthening of his resolution and self-reliance. And the higher he lifts his thoughts, the more manly, upright, and righteous he becomes, the greater will be his success, the more blessed and enduring will be his achievements.

The universe does not favor the greedy, the dishonest, the vicious, although on the mere surface it may sometimes appear to do so; it helps the honest, the magnanimous, the virtuous. All the great Teachers of the ages have declared this in varying forms, and to prove and know it a man has but to persist in making himself more and more virtuous by lifting up his thoughts.

Intellectual achievements are the result of thought consecrated to the search for knowledge, or for the beautiful and true in life and nature. Such achievements may be sometimes connected with vanity and ambition, but they are not the outcome of those characteristics; they are the natural outgrowth of long and arduous effort, and of pure and unselfish thoughts.

Spiritual achievements are the consummation of holy aspirations. He who lives constantly in the conception of noble and lofty thoughts, who dwells upon all that is pure and unselfish, will, as surely as the sun reaches its zenith and the moon its full, become wise and noble in character, and rise into a position of influence and blessedness.

Achievement, of whatever kind, is the crown of effort, the diadem of thought. By the aid of self-control, resolution, purity, righteousness, and well-directed thought a man ascends; by the aid of animality, indolence, impurity, corruption, and confusion of thought a man descends.

A man may rise to high success in the world, and even to lofty altitudes in the spiritual realm, and again descend into weakness and wretchedness by allowing arrogant, selfish, and corrupt thoughts to take possession of him.

Victories attained by right thought can only be maintained by watchfulness. Many give way when success is assured, and rapidly fall back into failure.

All achievements, whether in the business, intellectual, or spiritual world, are the result of definitely directed thought, are governed by the same law and are of the same method; the only difference lies in *the object of attainment.*

He who would accomplish little must sacrifice little; he who would achieve much must sacrifice much; he who would attain highly must sacrifice greatly.

Visions & Ideals

The dreamers are the saviors of the world. As the visible world is sustained by the invisible, so men, through all their trials and sins and sordid vocations, are nourished by the beautiful visions of their solitary dreamers. Humanity cannot forget its dreamers; it cannot let their ideals fade and die; it lives in them; it knows them as they *realities* which it shall one day see and know.

Composer, sculptor, painter, poet, prophet, sage, these are the makers of the after-world, the architects of heaven. The world is beautiful because they have lived; without them, laboring humanity would perish.

He who cherishes a beautiful vision, a lofty ideal in his heart, will one day realize it. Columbus cherished a vision of another world, and he discovered it; Copernicus fostered the vision of a multiplicity of worlds and a wider universe, and he revealed it; Buddha beheld the vision of a spiritual world of stainless beauty and perfect peace, and he entered into it.

Cherish your visions; cherish your ideals; cherish the music that stirs in your heart, the beauty that forms in your mind, the loveliness that drapes your purest thoughts, for out of them will grow all delightful conditions, all, heavenly environment; of these, if you but remain true to them, your world will at last be built.

To desire is to obtain; to aspire is to, achieve. Shall man's basest desires receive the fullest measure of gratification, and his purest aspirations starve for lack of sustenance? Such is not the Law: such a condition of things can never obtain: "ask and receive."

Dream lofty dreams, and as you dream, so shall you become. Your Vision is the promise of what you shall one day be; your Ideal is the prophecy of what you shall at last unveil.

The greatest achievement was at first and for a time a dream. The oak sleeps in the acorn; the bird waits in the egg; and in the highest vision of the soul a waking angel stirs. Dreams are the seedlings of realities.

Your circumstances may be uncongenial, but they shall not long remain so if you but perceive an Ideal and strive to reach it. You cannot travel *within* and stand still *without*. Here is a youth hard pressed by poverty and labor; confined long hours in an unhealthy workshop; unschooled, and lacking all the arts of refinement. But he dreams of better things; he thinks of intelligence, of refinement, of grace and beauty. He conceives of, mentally builds up, an ideal condition of life; the vision of a wider liberty and a larger scope takes possession of him; unrest urges him to action, and he utilizes all his spare time and means, small though they are, to the development of his latent powers and resources. Very soon so altered has his mind become that the workshop can no longer hold him. It has become so out of harmony with his mentality that it falls out of his life as a garment is cast aside, and, with the growth of opportunities, which fit the scope of his expanding powers, he passes out of it forever. Years later we see this youth as a full-grown man. We find him a master of certain forces of the mind, which he wields with worldwide influence and almost unequalled power. In his hands he holds the cords of gigantic responsibilities; he speaks, and lo, lives are changed; men and women hang upon his words and remold their characters, and, sunlike, he becomes the fixed and luminous center round which innumerable destinies revolve. He has realized the Vision of his youth. He has become one with his Ideal.

And you, too, youthful reader, will realize the Vision (not the idle wish) of your heart, be it base or beautiful, or a mixture of both, for you will always gravitate toward that which you, secretly, most love. Into your hands will be placed the exact results of your own thoughts; you will receive that which you earn; no more, no less. Whatever your present environment may be, you will fall, remain, or rise with your thoughts, your Vision, your Ideal. You will become as small as your controlling desire; as great as your dominant aspiration: in the beautiful words of Stanton Kirkham Davis, "You may be keeping accounts, and presently you shall walk out of the door that for so long has seemed to you the barrier of your ideals, and shall find yourself before an audience—the pen still behind your ear, the ink stains on your fingers and then and there shall pour out the torrent of your inspiration. You may be driving sheep, and you shall wander to the city-bucolic and open-mouthed; shall wander under the intrepid guidance of the spirit into the studio of the master, and after a time he shall say, 'I have nothing more to teach you.' And now you have become the master, who did so recently dream of great things while driving sheep. You shall lay down the saw and the plane to take upon yourself the regeneration of the world."

The thoughtless, the ignorant, and the indolent, seeing only the apparent effects of things and not the things themselves, talk of luck, of fortune, and chance. Seeing a man grow rich, they say, "How lucky he is!" Observing another become intellectual, they exclaim, "How highly favored he is!" And noting the saintly character and wide influence of another, they remark, "How chance aids him at every turn!" They do not see the trials and failures and struggles which these men have voluntarily encountered in order to gain their experience; have no knowledge of the sacrifices they have made, of the undaunted efforts they have put forth, of the faith they have exercised, that they might overcome the apparently insurmountable, and realize the Vision of their heart. They do not know the darkness and the heartaches; they only see the light and joy, and call it "luck". They do not see the long and arduous journey, but only behold the pleasant goal, and call it "good fortune," do not understand the process, but only perceive the result, and call it chance.

In all human affairs there are *efforts*, and there are *results*, and the strength of the effort is the measure of the result. Chance is not. Gifts, powers, material, intellectual, and spiritual possessions are the fruits of effort; they are thoughts completed, objects accomplished, visions realized.

The Vision that you glorify in your mind, the Ideal that you enthrone in your heart—this you will build your life by, this you will become.

Serenity

Calmness of mind is one of the beautiful jewels of wisdom. It is the result of long and patient effort in self-control. Its presence is an indication of ripened experience, and of a more than ordinary knowledge of the laws and operations of thought.

A man becomes calm in the measure that he understands himself as a thought evolved being, for such knowledge necessitates the understanding of others as the result of thought, and as he develops a right understanding, and sees more and more clearly the internal relations of things by the action of cause and effect he ceases to fuss and fume and worry and grieve, and remains poised, steadfast, serene.

The calm man, having learned how to govern himself, knows how to adapt himself to others; and they, in turn, reverence his spiritual strength, and feel that they can learn of him and rely upon him. The more tranquil a man becomes, the greater is his success, his influence, his power for good. Even the ordinary trader will find his business prosperity increase as he develops a greater self-control and equanimity, for people will always prefer to deal with a man whose demeanor is strongly equable.

The strong, calm man is always loved and revered. He is like a shade-giving tree in a thirsty land, or a sheltering rock in a storm. "Who does not love a tranquil heart, a sweet-tempered, balanced life? It does not matter whether it rains or shines, or what changes come to those possessing these blessings, for they are always sweet, serene, and calm. That exquisite poise of character, which we call serenity is the last lesson of culture, the fruitage of the soul. It is precious as wisdom, more to be desired than gold—yea, than even fine gold. How insignificant mere money seeking looks in comparison with a serene life—a life that dwells in the ocean of Truth, beneath the waves, beyond the reach of tempests, in the Eternal Calm!

"How many people we know who sour their lives, who ruin all that is sweet and beautiful by explosive tempers, who destroy their poise of character, and make bad blood! It is a question whether the great majority of people do not ruin their lives and mar their happiness by lack of self-control. How few people we meet in life who are well balanced, who have that exquisite poise which is characteristic of the finished character!

Yes, humanity surges with uncontrolled passion, is tumultuous with ungoverned grief, is blown about by anxiety and doubt only the wise man, only he whose thoughts are controlled and purified, makes the winds and the storms of the soul obey him.

Tempest-tossed souls, wherever ye may be, under whatsoever conditions ye may live, know this in the ocean of life the isles of Blessedness are smiling, and the sunny shore of your ideal awaits your coming. Keep your hand firmly upon the helm of thought. In the bark of your soul reclines the commanding Master; He does but sleep: wake Him. Self-control is strength; Right Thought is mastery; Calmness is power. Say unto your heart, "Peace, be still!"